STEAMING THROUGH West Sussex

Peter Hay

COVER PICTURE: One of the famous Brighton Atlantics, no. 32425 *Trevose Head*, takes water at Horsham on its way to Portsmouth with a special in May 1953.

Design – Deborah Goodridge

First published October 1987

ISBN 0 906520 50 9

© *Middleton Press, 1987*

Typeset by CitySet - Bosham 573270

Published by Middleton Press
Easebourne Lane
Midhurst, West Sussex
GU29 9AZ
☎ *073 081 3169*

Printed & bound by Biddles Ltd,
Guildford and Kings Lynn

CONTENTS

INDEX

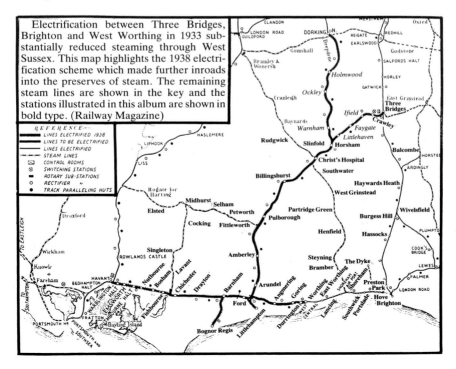

Electrification between Three Bridges, Brighton and West Worthing in 1933 substantially reduced steaming through West Sussex. This map highlights the 1938 electrification scheme which made further inroads into the preserves of steam. The remaining steam lines are shown in the key and the stations illustrated in this album are shown in bold type. (Railway Magazine)

INTRODUCTION

I have found too many interesting railway pictures taken in the county to confine my coverage of Sussex to a single volume and this one takes over where *Steaming Through East Sussex* leaves off. The county is therefore divided at the London - Brighton Main Line and there is a further selection of pictures of it, though this time I have started from the Brighton end. Next follows what used to be called the West Coast line, now the Coastway West, including the Cliftonville spur and branches to The Dyke, Littlehampton and Bognor. The rest of the lines in West Sussex are grouped (with doubtful logic) as listed in the Contents. Apart from the Cliftonville spur every line portrayed here has enjoyed more detailed coverage in previous Middleton Press books in the Southern Main Lines, South Coast Railways or Branch Line albums. There are also monographs by various authors on the Main and West Coast lines, the Dyke branch, and the Chichester - Midhurst line. The railways of Sussex are examined in a wider context in books by C.F. Dendy Marshall on the SR, and J.T. Howard Turner and C. Hamilton Ellis on the LBSCR. There are also more general books on the railways of southern England by H.P. White and Edwin Course.

Those sources explain the railway history in detail but for those who may not have access to them a brief summary of the story is this. Excepting the Midhurst - Petersfield section, all lines in West Sussex were built for or acquired before opening by the LBSCR. Brighton to Shoreham came first, then the Main Line from London. By the 1850s and 1860s the benefits of railway communication were so manifest that the county west of the Main Line was provided with lines, all of which developed their traffic only slowly. Chichester - Midhurst and the line to The Dyke are best described as semi-speculative ventures of the 1880s and the network was complete by 1887. In 1923 came the Grouping when the Southern Railway was formed by amalgamating the LBSCR with the LSWR to the west and the SECR to the east. The Southern electrified the West Coast and Mid-Sussex lines as well as the Main Line in the 1930s, a decade which saw the Dyke branch close completely and the Chichester - Midhurst line lose its passenger service. Increasing public preference for road vehicles killed the rest of the Midhurst lines in 1955 and the two branches from Christ's Hospital in the 1960s. There are no preserved lines in West Sussex though steam can still be enjoyed at the Chalk Pits Museum at Amberley.

As almost every picture has a steam engine in it somewhere, a few words of locomotive history may be useful. The Golden Age of the LBSCR began with William Stroudley's arrival at Brighton Works in 1870 and by 1900 few of his predecessors' engines survived. He was followed from 1889 by R.J. Billinton, D.E. Marsh, and finally Lawson Billinton, son of R.J. The Grouping ended the separate entity of the LBSCR Locomotive, Carriage and Wagon Department. SR designs by R.E.L. Maunsell and later O.V.S. Bulleid began to appear in Sussex. Rolling stock from the LSWR and SECR was also brought in as the older LBSCR equipment wore out. In steam's closing years BR provided LMS and its own standard types. A combination of electrification and the quality of LBSCR engineering however ensured that the native 'Brighton' article was still to be seen at work until the end of steam, many of the last examples still having years of life left in them when they ceased work at the diesel takeover. Scrapping steam eliminated the need for increasingly hard-to-staff depots for maintaining it. Happily an E4 class 0-6-2 tank is preserved on the Bluebell Railway; M7 class no. 30053 which appears in these pages has just returned from the USA, and several of Stroudley's 'Terrier' or A1X class 0-6-0 tanks have also escaped scrapping. Very few carriages or wagons have survived so these pictures must serve as their memorial.

As usual I have had more help than I deserve in bringing these pictures together and while it would be tedious to list everybody I cannot let this opportunity pass to render special thanks to J.H.W. (Joe) Kent, whom I met when I began taking railway photographs and who has helped me ever since. I must also mention the Railway Correspondence & Travel Society whose

History of LBSCR Locomotives has been most instructive, the Signalling Record Society which has provided information on signalling, and my fellow members of The Brighton Circle whose Circular unearths details we all thought lost for ever.

Lastly I must thank Norman Langridge and Godfrey Croughton for providing tickets from their collections and Neil Stanyon for reading the proofs and correcting my errors.

Where the descriptions in captions are inaccurate the fault is solely mine; where I have failed to point out something interesting in a picture you must decide whether I didn't notice it, didn't know what it was, or left it for you to spot for yourself.

Peter Hay
Hove 1987

Table 69 LONDON, PETERSFIELD, MIDHURST, PULBOROUGH, and LONDON
Third class only between Petersfield and Pulborough

1948

1 THE MAIN LINE: BRIGHTON TO THREE BRIDGES

The character of the London - Brighton line's southern end was a product of the geography of central Sussex and the state of railway technology when it was devised. By the late 1830s the cautious Stephensonian idea of avoiding the gradients at the expense of a longer route was being forsaken as Joseph Locke demonstrated the practicality of going up and over natural obstacles to direct routes. The hill climbing ability of locomotives was also improving rapidly. In 1837 Locke's Grand Junction Railway from Lancashire to Birmingham was opened with gradients which were considered steep. Sir John Rennie's route through Sussex was not so bold, but more direct than Stephenson's which would have followed the river valleys to Shoreham and entered Brighton from the west. Thus we have the Main Line as it is today, built under the supervision of John Urpeth Rastrick as engineer, with deep cuttings and long tunnels through the South Downs chalk and the sandstone of the Forest Ridge. And gradients: not a level yard in the county save in the platforms at Brighton.

The ruling gradient of 20 feet to the mile – 1 in 264 – starts at Brighton opposite the site of Montpelier Junction where the line to Lewes goes off over the viaduct. The first four miles are continuous uphill work for a 'cold' engine so steam trains from Brighton were often still only making a modest speed when they reached the top of the rise at the south end of Clayton tunnel. Many a down train, by contrast, has had a 'right time' arrival at Brighton only thanks to those four concluding downhill miles.

From Clayton tunnel going north, with the engine by now nicely warmed through, there follows an almost straight six miles downhill to north of Keymer Junction. It is excellent for getting a run at the eight mile pull up to Balcombe tunnel which follows, though often spoiled either by a signal check at Keymer Junction or a booked stop at Haywards Heath. On the climb to Balcombe tunnel what was a hindrance going north helped southbound trains and Haywards Heath station has witnessed some whirlwind flights of a Brighton Fast delayed in the London area. With a Fast, the golden rule was 'time at the Bridges and time at the Keymer'. Being on time at Three Bridges meant any delays further north had been recovered; if you were still on time at Keymer Junction things were going well on the engine, there were only another five miles uphill, and a punctual arrival at Brighton was 'in the bag'.

Apart from quadrupling through Three Bridges to Balcombe Tunnel Junction and some realignments in the Brighton area, Rastrick would still recognise his route if he could rise from that massive tomb in Brighton Cemetery. The stations by architect David Mocatta he would find greatly changed. Indeed these pictures show much that has been lost in the last 30 years, by way of buildings and their amenities. Steam itself is gone of course and today the electrics and diesels make light of that 'cold start' up the bank from Brighton station.

LOCAL TRAFFIC.

(139)

London Brighton & South Coast Rly.

From BRIGHTON

To Three Bridges (Up Siding)

Truck No. 10864

Date July 9 1909

Consignee per Petrie

1. After its second reversal, the Hastings - Birkenhead through train leaves Brighton bound for Redhill. In July 1955 the engine is D class 4–4–0 no. 31734 which has arrived here on a train from Tonbridge. The carriages are pre-war SR vintage, painted red and cream by their new owners and roof boarded for this working. Tomorrow there will be GWR stock heading north at this time. On the right there is a Stroudley water crane, a hand-operated trolley to replenish train lavatory tanks, and some schoolboys who have turned their backs on the Bulleid Pacific heading the 11.00 am to Cardiff.

2. In 1957 the bulk of the locomotive works dominated the east side of Brighton station as it had for a century, and its shunting engine, just seen on the left, enlivened the local railway scene. Alas today, they are both just memories like L class no. 31766 and the flat-sided Maunsell coaches leaving for Tonbridge.

3. The inside of the main Erecting Shop seen in the previous picture, where engine building and repair continued well into the 1950s. Prominent are M7 class 0–4–4 tank no. 30057 with E2 class 0–6–0 tank no. 32103 beyond. Further back there are BR and SR engines while on the floor in front of the E2, the Drummond dome and Urie stovepipe chimney of a T9 class wait to be reinstated.

4. This is 'Nightmare Corner' at the top of the Cliftonville spur. In April 1953 E4 class 0–6–2 tank no. 32511 seems to be coping well with the mid-morning transfer goods from Hove to Brighton Top Yard, identified by having a brake van at the front as well as the rear. (J.H.W. Kent)

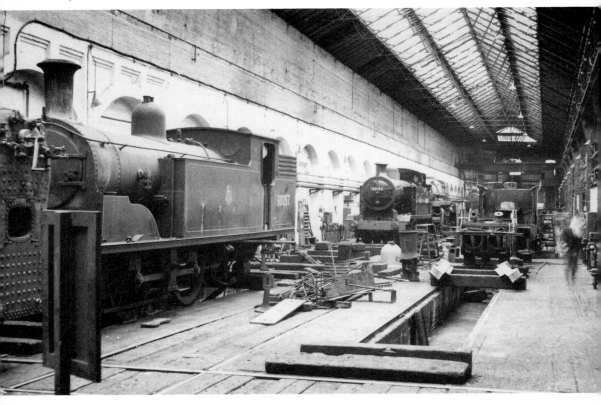

5. Another view of the Birkenhead - Hastings through train, southbound through Preston Park this time. In April 1952 BR influence is confined to renumbering the engine and painting *BRITISH RAILWAYS* on the tender. The coaches are still in SR colours while the engine goes one better: L1 class no. 31789 has the lovely malachite green livery with full black and yellow lining.

6. Although his train is still on the 1 in 264 up
grade to the south portal of Clayton tunnel,
the driver of the 11.05 am Walsall to Hastings
has such confidence in Brighton Altantic
no. 32422 *North Foreland* that he has shut off

steam after passing Hassocks station in the distance. The white blob by the end of the train is a water tower for goods train engines waiting in the sidings for a pathway into Brighton.

7. The characteristics of Hudson's Sand siding are referred to in the Middleton Press *Three Bridges to Brighton* album and this 1923 picture shows E2 class no. 109 passing under the arch which still exists, carrying the A273 road. The gradients of the siding are obvious. It seems to have closed in the 1920s.

8. A much older and closer view of the south end of Hassocks station showing a down stopping train in the charge of a D1 class 0–4–2 tank, standing beside the 1875 signal box which was well elevated to get a view of down trains over the wide platform awning. (Brighton Library)

9. On 25th May 1913 the signal box seen in the previous picture was replaced by this one, on the Brighton side of the road bridge this time. After the pre-war electrification and resignalling it was only opened for shunting movements into the down sidings and the goods yard opposite, so there is no signalman to observe the thunderous passage of Schools class 4–4–0 no. 30902 *Wellington* racing up the main line in July 1960. (J.H.W. Kent)

L. B. & S. C. RY
Available on the **DATE** of issue **ONLY**.
This Ticket is issued subject to the Regulations & Conditions stated in the Company's Time Tables & Bills
BURGESS HILL
TO
WIVELSFIELD wi.
1d. THIRD CLASS. 1d.
5347 3347

London Brighton & South Coast Railway

Southwater to

Three Bridges

10. A Maunsell Mogul darkens the sky at Hassocks in the summer of 1960 as it bustles north with a through train to the Western Region. Of the station, we can see the curious '1½' awnings over the extra wide platform and a glimpse of Mocatta's original buildings behind the engine. (J.H.W. Kent)

11. The Burgess Hill signal box was probably provided, like the one at Hassocks, in 1913, replacing an earlier structure which straddled the siding connection line on the right. A Brighton Mogul, K class no. 32338, is making good time on the up line to avoid delay to the frequent electric services. (J.H.W. Kent)

12. Comparison with picture 6 in *Steaming Through East Sussex* and the sequence in the *Three Bridges to Brighton* album will show how slowly things changed at Burgess Hill station. Electric light came after this 1960 scene with a Maunsell N class 2–6–0 passing through under the watchful eye of the Station Master. No Saturday half day for *him*. (J.H.W. Kent)

13. This is approximately the view of Keymer Junction that signalmen had until 1912 when a new box was built immediately to the right of the engine. By 1955 only a depression in the bank marked its position. The engine is D1 class 4–4–0 no. 31727 on its way from Brighton to Redhill.

14. At the head of a northbound Inter-Regional Saturday train passing Wivelsfield, U1 class no. 31890 has ample steam as it begins the climb to Balcombe tunnel. Larger splashers and dropped footplating made this engine unique in its class, having been rebuilt from a three cylinder 2–6–4 tank in 1928. (J.H.W. Kent)

15. The Hastings - Birkenhead train overtook a Seaford to Horsted Keynes electric at Haywards Heath each morning by running non-stop through the up loop. The driver of D1 class 4–4–0 no. 31492 on 10th October 1957 has shut off steam for the divergence onto the loop at the south end of the station, causing the safety valves to lift.

16. In 1963 Haywards Heath still had a goods yard and shed on the down side. The yard closed in 1970 but the goods shed was only demolished in 1987, to make way for a motor car service station. Happily the Liverpool Arms – 'Nadler & Collyers Entire' – survived. The engine of this Engineer's train is Q1 class 0–6–0 no. 33015. (J.H.W. Kent)

17. While the 1960s brought changes in the steam engines and their carriages on the Main Line, the electric scene was still firmly rooted in the 1930s, as the 4LAV leaving the down platform shows. On the up line there is a BR train: Standard 4–6–0 no. 75075 and new carriages. Spot the misplaced headcode disc. (J.H.W. Kent)

18. The railtour shown in picture 3 of *Steaming Through East Sussex* made a diversion to Horsted Keynes after arriving from London and here we see it pulling up the 1 in 85 to rejoin the Main Line at Copyhold Junction on its return. The date is 1962 and the engine is an ex-GNR saddle tank. (J.H.W. Kent)

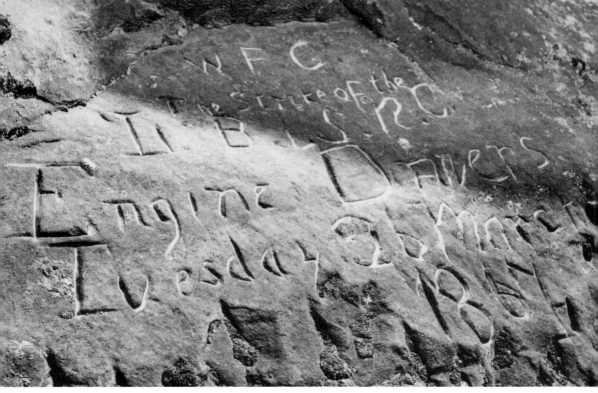

19. By September 1957 no. 32424 *Beachy Head* was the last 4–4–2 or Atlantic type engine at work in Britain, and moreover still working on the line for which it was built. On this occasion the Saturday Leicester to Hastings train was favoured by such distinguished haulage, here crossing the Ouse Viaduct. Let us hope there was a railway enthusiast on board to savour the event.

20. This inscription in the sandstone above the down platform at Balcombe reads: "W F C The Strike of the L.B.S.C.R. Engine Drivers. Tuesday 26 March 1867". Although the stone is soft this must have taken some time to cut, and it has been suggested that enginemen stopped their trains wherever they were at midnight on the appointed day and remained immobile for the whole 24 hours. (J.H.W. Kent)

21. For this 1964 excursion from the London Midland Region Northampton shed has turned out a polished 'Black 5' no. 45022, which is seen running fast on the descent through Balcombe station. The BR lamp headcode for a through passenger train has been used, rather than the SR disc headcode and the number 1X84 identifies the actual train for signalmen. Carriages are BR. (J.H.W. Kent)

22. Stroudley goods tank no. 116 *Touraine* (E1 class) from Tunbridge Wells resting at Three Bridges at the end of a siding on the up side beside the Crawley to East Grinstead road about 1900. Although the condition of the paintwork would indicate that overhaul and repainting has recently occurred, the big end of one of the inside connecting rods sticking out of the cab doorway suggests that *Touraine* was still suffering from some internal malady.

23. Among the sadder changes of 1987 is the demolition of the overall roof covering the former East Grinstead bay platform, on the right in this 1930s picture. In fact this Three Bridges to Tunbridge Wells train is starting from the Down Fast line platform, behind E4 class 0–6–2 tank no. B518. (H.C. Casserley)

2 THE WEST COAST LINE

The line westwards to Shoreham was Brighton's first railway, opened with band and ceremony on 11th May 1840, well over a year before the line from London. Hove was then centred on the Manor House and the old church; one early railway plan had the fashionable district adjoining the sea front west of Brighton served by a terminating branch from the Shoreham line. In fact Hove's first station at the top of Holland Road was a modest affair and did not prosper, for the town developed further west under the name of Cliftonville. The new station of 1865 recognised this growth and its name, so by 1880 the first station was defunct.

Westwards towards Chichester building followed the railway. Today there is scarcely a yard of the coast between Brighton and Littlehampton which is not built upon, while the fertile soils of the widening coastal plain have gradually experienced a change in use which owes a lot to the railway. Fields and pastures have given way to housing and market gardens. The latter owe their growth directly to cheap, mass-produced glass and the railway services which for several generations took their produce overnight to the London markets.

West of the river Arun the line changes character. The sea is further away – Littlehampton and Bognor are served by branches built in the 1860s – and there is farmland on both sides of the line. Beyond Chichester we are again in the region of 'Motor Halts', a feature of a semi-suburban landscape. They appeared in 1905 between Brighton and West Worthing and, being successful, were provided between Chichester and Portsmouth the following year. From Chichester to the county boundary the railway is close to the main east - west road which has always had small settlements along it, so the semi-suburban pattern seen from the carriage window east of the Arun is repeated here.

There were two exceptions to the extremely easy gradients of the West Coast line, one of them the lost and much lamented Dyke branch. It is reviewed at length in the *Brighton to Worthing* album (Middleton Press 1983) and also in Paul Clark's book *The Railways of the Devil's Dyke* (Turntable Publications 1976). The other line where gradients were a problem has found no such fame. Until 1879 trains between London and the West Coast line had to reverse at Brighton, a great nuisance, but in that year the Cliftonville spur was opened from Preston Park to the line between Hove and Cliftonville stations. Note the names: the present Hove station remained Cliftonville & West Brighton until 1893. The Spur, as it is known locally, is steeply graded throughout. There is a sharp curve at each end with a tunnel near the top for good measure. Preston Park's home signal is exactly at the top of the climb, so any up train stopped by it has its whole length on the grade and also round the sharp curve. For this reason the signalman at Hove East was not in my time allowed to send a train up the Spur until he had 'line clear' from Preston Park. Horror stories of engines stopped at the top of the bank being totally unable to get going again are evidence that this rule did not always exist. As well as the London - Worthing passenger service the Spur saw lots of goods train because, until the late 1950s, Hove had a small marshalling yard. To avoid congesting Brighton station, traffic to and from Brighton Top Yard (on the main line opposite Lovers' Walk Traction Maintenance Depot) went via the Spur and Preston Park. In the 1940s we schoolboys used to crawl through the fence at the end of the playing fields and sit above the Hove end of Cliftonville tunnel, just to see the Hove pilot engine bringing the last transfer goods of the day up the hill. In the warm summer dusk it was the 5th of November every night, with the occasional repeat performance if the engine stalled in the cutting below us and had to retreat to Hove Yard for a second attempt. Today the diesels and the electric engines treat the Spur with disdain, as if it was flat.

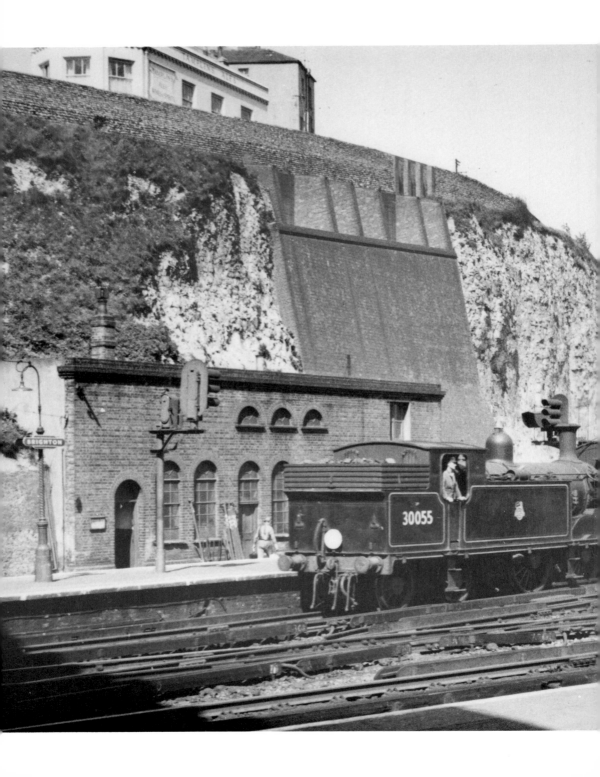

24. This view of a Sunday morning train from Horsham arriving at Brighton was taken from the main line platforms. The scene is much less congested than picture 13 in the *Brighton to Worthing* album and the layout has been further simplified since it was taken in May 1957. M7 class no. 30055 is hauling a 1921 SECR 10 compartment third coupled to a much older LSWR brake.

25. New England Road bridge at Brighton is the gateway to the West Coast line and through it has just passed another train from Horsham which, apart from the SR van in the centre, is pure LBSCR. Of the engines in sight, only an LMS-type 2–6–4 tank tells us that this is 1953 and not many years earlier.

26. The West Coast line profited greatly from the 'Motor Halts' of 1905/6, but Holland Road succumbed to bus competition in 1956. After the 1933 electrification few steam trains called there. The up side platform, all in timber, was virtually unchanged since 1905. Yet another Horsham - Brighton train appears, behind no. 32586 which was one of the rare E5X class 0–6–2 tanks.

27. A 15 chain radius curve on an incline of 1 in 90 means that K class no. 32348 is having to call on its considerable power to lift this Hove to Norwood goods up the Cliftonville Spur in August 1952. The 50¼ mile post (from London Bridge) is in the foreground with Hove East signal box home signals on the left.

28. An overhead view of the east end of Hove's layout before the recent track alterations simplified the junction with the Spur. The train passing Hove East signal box (later Hove A and finally just Hove) is the 1.50 pm Bournemouth West to Brighton, unusually worked by T9 class 4–4–0 no. 30728, rare in 1956 though common on this line before the war.

29. In 1957 Hove was the western boundary of the Brighton area colour light signalling so Hove East home signal has a 3-position colour light underneath giving advance notice of line occupation all the way to the terminus. It is Sunday evening and the Q class 0–6–0 is working a return excursion to Reading via Horsham. On the right is a side and end loading dock, much used when Hove passengers took their horses and carriages with them on long journeys.

30. In March 1958 a 'Transport Treasures' exhibition was held in the down sidings west of Hove station, the most notable exhibit being LSWR T3 class no. 563, today housed in the National Railway Museum. I wonder if these children remember 'going on the engine'. These sidings, like the brewery malt-houses behind, have long since been removed.

31. M7 class no. 30053 has also escaped the breaker's yard and in 1987 returned from a 20-year stay in the USA. How fine if the Swanage Railway could return it to working order so that it could pull out of Hove once again with a Horsham train. Alas it wouldn't get beyond Beeding Cement works.

32. Although allowed slightly more time than the electrics, the Brighton - Horsham steam trains had to maintain a brisk pace between Brighton and Shoreham. H class 0–4–4 tank no. 31310 is accelerating past Aldrington Halt (once Dyke Junction Halt) with a 2-coach LBSCR 'motor' set in December 1953. Notice how rebuilding in concrete has created a semi-staggered arrangement of platforms compared with the original motor halt.

33. A general view of The Dyke station with a train approaching from Brighton about 1910. The most permanent-looking structure is the signal box, corrugated iron being the standard building material at The Dyke. (Lens of Sutton)

BRIGHTON AND DYKE.—RAIL MOTOR SERVICE.

· Single Line between Dyke Junction and Dyke.   The Train Staff Stations are Hove and Dyke.

DOWN.—WEEK DAYS.

		Mixed a.m.	a.m.	p.m.	p.m.	p.m.										
M.C.	Brighton .... dep.	10 0	11 3	12 45	2 37	4 40	...	...	...	...	...	...	...	...	...
...	Holland Road Halt... ,,	10 3	11 6	12 48	2 40	4 43	...	...	...	...	...	...	...	...	...
0 70	Hove .... { arr.	10 5	11 9	12 51	2 43	4 46	...	...	...	...	...	...	...	...	...
1 34	.... { dep.	10 10													
2 2	Dyke Junction Halt ,,	10 12	11 11	12 53	2 45	4 48	...	...	...	...	...	...	...	...	...
5 49	The Dyke............... arr.	10 25	11 23	1 5	2 57	5 0	...	...	...	...	...	...	...	...	...

DOWN.—SUNDAYS, CHRISTMAS DAY AND GOOD FRIDAY.

	a.m.	a.m.	p.m.	p.m.										
Brighton .... dep.	10 0	11 15	2 40	4 30	...	...	...	...	...	...	...	...	...	...
Holland Road Halt... ,,	10 3	11 18	2 43	4 33	...	...	...	...	...	...	...	...	...	...
Hove .... ,,	10 6	11 21	2 46	4 36	...	...	...	...	...	...	...	...	...	...
Dyke Junction Halt ,,	10 8	11 23	2 48	4 38	...	...	...	...	...	...	...	...	...	...
The Dyke............... arr.	10 20	11 35	3 0	4 50	...	...	...	...	...	...	...	...	...	...

UP.—WEEK DAYS.

		Mixed a.m.	a.m.	p.m.	p.m.	p.m.										
M.C.	The Dyke........... dep.	10 48	11 28	1 15	4 15	5 10	...	...	...	...	...	...	...	...	...
...	Dyke Junction Halt ,,	...	11 39	1 26	4 26	5 21	...	...	...	...	...	...	...	...	...
3 47	Hove .... { arr.	11 4	11 41	1 28	4 28	5 23	...	...	...	...	...	...	...	...	...
4 15	.... { dep.	11 6													
4 53	Holland Road Halt ... ,,	...	11 43	1 30	4 30	5 25	...	...	...	...	...	...	...	...	...
5 49	Brighton .... arr.	11 10	11 47	1 34	4 34	5 29	...	...	...	...	...	...	...	...	...

UP.—SUNDAYS, CHRISTMAS DAY AND GOOD FRIDAY.

	a.m.	p.m.	p.m.	p.m.										
The Dyke............... dep.	10 30	1 5	4 0	5 15	...	...	...	...	...	...	...	...	...	...
Dyke Junction Halt ,,	10 41	1 16	4 11	5 26	...	...	...	...	...	...	...	...	...	...
Hove .... ,,	10 43	1 18	4 13	5 28	...	...	...	...	...	...	...	...	...	...
Holland Road Halt... ,,	10 45	1 20	4 16	5 30	...	...	...	...	...	...	...	...	...	...
Brighton .... arr.	10 49	1 24	4 19	5 34	...	...	...	...	...	...	...	...	...	...

Dyke Golf Club Private Halt.—Drivers are required to pass this Halt at a speed not exceeding 5 miles per hour, and to be prepared to stop to take up or set down passengers as required.   (T.R. 14762/14 T.T.)

34. The E1 class heavy goods tank was not the commonest type used on the Dyke services, though its '6-wheel drive' would be a great help with the first working up on a frosty morning. The skyline beyond gives an idea of the uphill walk that greeted passengers who wished to get to the crest of the Downs. (Lens of Sutton)

35. A broadside view of the Sentinel steam railcar with which in 1933 the Southern Railway tried to reduce expenses on the Dyke branch. Despite its 'Bennie Railplane' appearance, it was no flyer except when the brakes overheated going down the 1 in 40 to the coast. Eventually it worked itself out of a job because sometimes there were just too many passengers, and proper trains reappeared until the end came in 1938. (H.C. Casserley)

36. Portslade was one of the first level crossings on the Coastway West to have lifting barriers, but the traditional gates were still in use in September 1957. Notice the signal box, a typical Saxby & Farmer product from about 1880, of which the LBSCR had many dozens. The M7 class tank is no. 30050.

37. The houses are beginning to creep out towards Fishersgate in this Edwardian view of a London - Worthing train, taken from the footbridge before the halt was opened. On the north side, the railwaymen's allotments are bounded only by a hedge though a fence has appeared on the south side. (Brighton Library)

38. Fifty years later railwaymen still cultivated the lineside, but the hedge and the allotments beyond have been replaced by a fence, gardens, and houses. Suburbia has arrived and so has a two lever ground frame controlling access to an electricity grid switching station. The Brighton to Bournemouth train, strengthened to eight coaches on a Saturday, is hauled by one of Brighton's L class 4-4-0s, no. 31776.

39. A closer look at M7 tank no. 30049 from Horsham, as it hurries by the CEGB switching station created to distribute the output of the two power stations situated beside the beach, ½ mile to the south. The fact that many of the Horsham and Brighton trains included a van shows how, as late as 1953, the railway was a vital part of the country transport network, carrying more prams, parcels, and mails than the Guard's van could hold.

40. When the remote control 'motor train' gear fitted to pre-Grouping engines wore out in the 1950s, new sets were not considered worth making, BR using a vacuum-operated arrangement as against the LBSCR/SR compressed air type. The coaches also were nearing the end of their life, so trains like this one at Southwick often replaced the previous pull and push workings. Class E4 0–6–2 tank no. 32494 is hauling an SECR 'Birdcage' set in April 1956, the pre-Grouping trio being completed by the 2NOL electric on the down line, LSWR steam stock fitted with electric motors.

42. The Lancing Carriage Works train, also known as 'The Lancing Belle', brought staff down from Brighton in the morning and took them home after work. Here, double headed to avoid delaying electric trains over the gently rising section of line between the Adur and Brighton, it pulls away from Shoreham, with the goods yard on the left and the station in the background. The engines in September 1953 are C class 0–6–0 no. 31270 and E4 no. 32566.

41. Rather than entering the sea directly, the river Adur flows eastwards past Shoreham to an outlet at Kingston Buci in Southwick where there was a rail-connected tidal wharf. The P class 0–6–0 tanks were the last steam engines to work there regularly, until 1959. The screw coupling at the front of the engine gave the wagon attached by it an easier passage round the sharp curves of these sidings.

43. With a steady falling gradient from Brighton, the eleven old LSWR carriages of 'The Lancing Belle' could be managed unaided by an E4 tank in the morning. Shoreham's nameboard was still LBSCR in 1956, metal letters screwed on a matchboard backing.

44. 'The First Wagon Lancing 13 April '09' is the inscription on this contemporary photograph. It conflicts with published statements that the Works did not begin operations until 1912, but they may refer to carriage construction.

The First Wagon Lancing 13 April '09

45. It appears that 'The Lancing Belle' first ran in 1919 and this picture may show the carriages which were initially provided. They were built for London suburban services in 1895-97. At Lancing they were replaced by the 1940s with those shown in picture 42. In 1930 the engine in charge, as for so many years, was an E4 'Radial' tank, no. B480. (Brighton Library)

46. The 'Motor Halts' of 1905 did not contain the word Halt on the platform nameboards though it was used in the timetable. Ham Bridge remained thus until renamed East Worthing Halt in 1949. This 1920s view shows a Brighton to Portsmouth train hurrying through behind a B4 class 4–4–0. (Lens of Sutton)

47. The 11.00 am Brighton to Cardiff train slowing to its first stop, at Worthing, in February 1957. The gleaming West Country class Pacific is no. 34048 *Crediton*, passing a K class waiting patiently for permission to regain the running line after shunting Worthing goods yard. Recent property development has completely obliterated the goods yard site.

48. A goods train pulling out of the up loop at Worthing in February 1957 behind K class no. 32344. The goods shed siding on the extreme left did not carry engines and had lost each alternate sleeper.

LOCAL PARCEL: PAID.

London Brighton & South Coast Rly.
(22 674)

TO
ARUNDEL

FROM WORTHING

49. The man in shirt sleeves and bow tie may be a clerk at Worthing station, but his heavy apron and the open cab door on the engine suggest he belongs to the Locomotive Department and is engaged on some technical business on Atlantic no. 426. The Driver is on his seat, a wooden platform on top of the screw reversing gear. (Brighton Library)

50. Another view of the west end of Worthing station, between 1933 and 1938 when the electrics completed their takeover of the West Coast line and steam motor trains were no longer needed beyond West Worthing. D1 class 0–4–2 tank no. 2605 is pulling two of the high roofed 'Balloon' carriages dating from 1905/6. (Brighton Library)

51. No. 37 was the first of the popular Brighton Atlantics (class H1), here seen leaving West Worthing with a Brighton to Portsmouth train after its first repaint in 1909. All the carriages are of the low roofed Billinton design which preceded Marsh's 'Balloon' type. (E. R. Lacey collection)

52. Twenty years later and one of the handsome Baltic tanks, no. B329 *Stephenson*, heads the 5.55 pm London Bridge to Bognor through West Worthing. The setting sun just reaches the north side of the train, letting us see the up side buildings as well. (Lens of Sutton)

53. Its new white concrete still unsullied by engine smoke, the road bridge at Durrington frames an I3 class 4–4–2 tank on a Brighton to Portsmouth train in 1936. Work has not yet begun on building Durrington station but rails and sleepers of the SR pattern are lying waiting to replace the LBSCR ones in the foreground. (Brighton Library)

L. B. & S. C. Ry.
Available on the **DATE** of issue **ONLY**
This Ticket is issued subject to the Regulations, & Conditions stated in the Company's Time Tables & Bills.

4479

CHICHESTER
TO
WORTHING WO 4479

1s. ⌐⌐ Third Class. 1s.5½d.

ROUNDSTONE

80017

54. LBSCR rolling stock from the late Victorian years disappeared quite quickly under the SR regime in the 1920s, being replaced on secondary services like this Portsmouth to Brighton train by LSWR carriages. The engine about to come under the eye of the Goring signalman is a reboilered T9 class 4–4–0 similar to the one in picture 28. (Brighton Library)

55. Although fitted with 'electrification flashes', BR Standard 2–6–4 tank no. 80017 was unlikely to meet any overhead wires on the West Coast line in April 1964 and certainly not at Roundstone Crossing between Goring and Angmering. (J.H.W. Kent)

56. The Driver's view up the line from the footplate of Q class 0–6–0 no. 30531 was somewhat obscured on a chill spring morning in 1964 as he passed through Angmering. On the platform beside the engine there are barrowloads of hothouse produce, always an important traffic at this station. Comparison with the pictures in the *Worthing to Chichester* album shows that the crossover has been repositioned beyond the level crossing and ahead of the starting signal. A subsidiary signal has therefore been provided for movements going only as far as the crossover. (J.H.W. Kent)

57. With the locomotive yard opposite the platform, Littlehampton was a good place for posed pictures of engines, generally with the houses in Gloucester Road as a background. This is E5 class no. 594 *Shortbridge* from New Cross shed in London, probably about 1908 before the name and elaborate lining were discontinued. (Brighton Library)

58. Another picture of that memorable day in 1920 when D1 tank no. 360 attempted to escape the confines of the station at Littlehampton. Apart from the boiler-suited workmen engaged on rerailing the runaway, half the town is looking on from the road outside. Despite having demolished the buffer stops and being somewhat 'down by the head' in naval parlance, the spare engine lamps are still securely in place on their tank-top brackets. (Brighton Library)

60. This picture of Ford bridge was taken from the site of the wharf beside the Arun which was opened in 1850, connecting with the West Coast line at the east end of Ford station. By May 1956, when this eastbound goods appeared headed by Q class no. 30544, the wharf and its connection were long disused though the trespass noticeboard still stood.

London Brighton and South Coast Railway.

Littlehampton Har. to

Bramber

59. The pattern of tracks on Littlehampton wharf in February 1956 deserves close study. In the foreground is an ordinary quayside siding. The rail beyond ends in a bolted-on metal block, and is one of the tracks for the nearer crane. The next two rails are a siding passing beneath the crane, then there is another crane track, and lastly a siding with Terrier no. 32661, the only class of engine allowed on the decayed wharves by this date.

61. The wharf connection goes off on the right in this 1912 picture of the eastern approach to Ford station, complete with the first signal box, a Saxby & Farmer construction of 1863. Ford Junction signal box and its up home signals beyond the bridge can be seen in the far distance behind the Victoria to Portsmouth train, which is headed by no. 24, an I3 class 4–4–2 tank. (Brighton Library)

62. For operating reasons this long goods train has been stabled (never 'parked') in the refuge siding at the west end of Ford station. Now K class no. 32352 from Three Bridges shed has arrived to take it forward to Brighton. By May 1956 the station had lost all its suffixes and was just plain Ford though the platform nameboard was once more informative.

63. A distant view of the west end of Ford station in May 1956 as 'Vulcan' goods no. 32522 rumbles through with the afternoon goods off the Mid-Sussex line.

64. The LBSCR Royal Train approaches Barnham Junction from the east on 29th January 1901. King Edward VII is just one week into his reign but the engine is not carrying the full panoply of the Royal Arms as the King is not on board. The B4 class 4–4–0 is probably bringing some foreign sovereign to Portsmouth en route to Osborne on the Isle of Wight where Queen Victoria had died a week earlier.
(E.R. Lacey collection)

London Brighton & South Coast Railway.

Barnham Junction to

Selham

65. The up starting signal on the left locates this view at exactly the same spot as the previous one, 26 years later. Even the type of engine is the same, a B4 class 4–4–0, no. B65. The structure identified on the 1912 map as a signal box has been swept away with the lengthening of the down platform, almost certainly as part of the alterations which allowed through running onto the Bognor branch. On 26th February 1927, five years after the grouping, the whole scene is still LBSCR. There is no visible sign of the Southern Railway. (H.C. Casserley)

67. Major accidents get photographed, but we rarely see pictures of those minor troubles which just make life difficult. The left hand crankpin of this C2 class 0–6–0 has overheated on the road and during a stop at Barnham the fireman is giving first aid by pouring water on the afflicted part of no. B552. Give thanks to H.M. Madgwick for having his camera at the ready.

66. The west end of Barnham Junction is seen about 1890, when slotted post signals with separate rotating lamps were still in use, ballast still covered the sleepers, and the locomotives of Stroudley's predecessor J.C. Craven still worked the quieter parts of the LBSCR. (Lens of Sutton)

68. A train from London enters Bognor on 2nd October 1937 with I3 class no. 2025 hauling set 472, built by the SR in 1926. The fine wooden signal gantry at the approach to the station was removed when a new signal box was provided as part of the 1938 electrification works. (H.C. Casserley)

69. The Bognor branch train stands at the terminus about 1900, with the 1876 signal box on the left. Terrier no. 43 *Gipsyhill* has a fine collection of four-wheeled gaslit 'bouncers' in tow, through the guard in the front van has only an oil lamp for illumination. (Brighton Library)

70. B2X class 4–4–0 no. 321 was the pride of Bognor shed in the last years of the LBSCR and here, with paint and brightwork polished, it is pulling out with the only through train of the day to London, at 8.10 am. (E.R. Lacey collection)

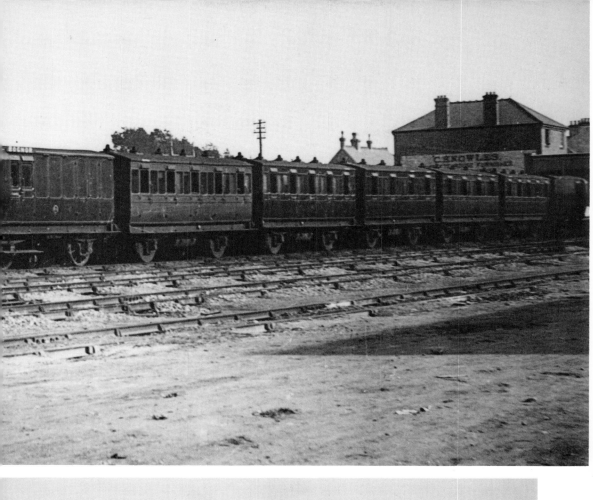

71. Apart from repainting and fitting of the vacuum brake the B4 class 4–4–0s were little altered by the Southern Railway in its early years. No. B74 was working the 1.27pm Portsmouth Harbour to London Bridge in the late 1920s, here passing Drayton station, which closed to passengers on 1st June 1930. As well as the engine, most of the train is LBSCR stock of the Billinton era. (E.R. Lacey collection)

72. Chichester East signal box was renamed Chichester A by BR and in March 1964 the signalman witnessed the melancholy sight of steam for scrap, as N class Moguls nos. 31830 and 31832 made their last journey behind class 33 no. D6545. To reduce the burden on underline bridges they were separated by empty coal wagons. (J.H.W. Kent)

73. A high level view of the Brighton - Plymouth train in April 1964, seen from the windows of Chichester West (or B) signal box. Behind Class 4 2–6–4 tank no. 80014 are the extensive pens once used for loading cattle in connection with Chichester market, a traffic which now goes by road. (J.H.W. Kent)

74. In September 1964 rebuilt West Country class no. 34025 *Whimple* leaves Chichester going under clear signals. The one on the right applies to the line on the left of it which was electrified to accommodate the Bulleid/Raworth Co-Co electric locomotives which relinquished westbound goods trains at this point. (J.H.W. Kent)

75. The leading wagons of this Salisbury to Chichester goods are passing over the connection to the Midhurst line, shown in picture 108. There is a mixed load behind U class no. 31790, with a cattle wagon as the second vehicle and some high-capacity mineral wagons further down the train. (J.H.W. Kent)

76. Chichester was for many years the interchange point between the Western and Central sections of the SR, goods trains being remarshalled and changing engines, so the LSWR type S15 class 4–6–0s normally came off there, using the triangle to turn before returning westwards. No. 30834 was one of the batch built by the SR in 1927 and was within two months of withdrawal when this picture was taken in September 1964. (J.H.W. Kent)

77. Your author helped to site the Pullman Camping Coach at Bosham but was unable to penetrate the mysteries of an 'automatic self-emptying cesspool' which he was told the station possessed, when trying to sort out sewerage for the Pullman. Subsequent happenings are best not referred to. Another S15 passes through on the up line in May 1964. (J.H.W. Kent)

78. The signal box at Bosham was one of the final LBSCR pattern and probably dates from the rebuilding of the station in 1902-04, the previous box standing east of the level crossing. Heading for Brighton is BR class 4 2–6–0 no. 76068 with a short departmental train in April 1964. (J.H.W. Kent)

79. A Motor Car Halt was opened in 1906 at Broad Road Crossing (no.62 gates) to serve the village of Nutbourne on the main road nearby. As the Terrier prepares to propel its 'Balloon' towards Portsmouth there are lots of things worth study. The circle on the house carries its number: 62; the wicket gate has a notice about trespass, while a timetable board has been screwed to the crossing gates. The oval plate beside it bids travellers to Ring the Bell if they wish the gates opened. (Lens of Sutton)

80. Lacking a picture of steam at Southbourne, let us admire *Southbourne*, the last Stroudley 'single'. An unusual feature visible is the small disc wheel below the framing under the Westinghouse pump. It is connected to a boss on the driving axle by a cord, by which Stroudley's patent speed indicator is made to function. *Southbourne* was built at Brighton in 1882 for £2765 and lasted until 1908. (Brighton Library)

3. MID-SUSSEX

The LBSCR referred to the route through Horsham and the Arun valley as the Mid-Sussex Direct Line. Thus the heading of the London - Portsmouth service timetable, worded with the competing LSWR Portsmouth Direct line in mind. Despite these pretensions the section between Horsham and Arundel must have been pretty much of a backwater in steam days. Pulborough for instance saw its last up train of the day depart at 8.45 pm and residents who wanted an evening in Town had to sleep there because the last down train for the Mid-Sussex line left Victoria at 7.25 pm.

Electrification in 1938 changed life on the Mid-Sussex, probably more than anywhere else in Sussex. From a steam pattern of roughly one train each way about every 1½ hours, the staff had to adjust themselves to three times as many services. Only the Midhurst branch timetable remained unmoved by this earthquake. Another novelty which arrived with the electrics was the so-called 'tick-stop', the timetable clerks' name for what became the norm on electrified routes. In steam days no train was timed to spend less than a full minute at a station, with separate arrival and departure times shown in the timetable. The electrics were only allowed 20 seconds for a station stop unless a longer duration was expressly shown. *Twenty seconds*! Some of the 'old brigade' took about that long to stop what they were doing and get out on the platform. Yet it worked. How we would like to have a vernacular account of what the change felt like to the men whose railway had run at a country rhythm. Of course Herbert Walker, the Southern Railway's great electrifying General Manager was right: the 'Spark Effect' touched even the Mid-Sussex line, and the traffic grew. It took time though and even in the 1950s the stations in the Arun valley felt more like those on say the Oxted line than those along the coast. If they hadn't been electrified they might well have been closed in the Beeching years.

I ought to mention a Mid-Sussex marvel of LBSCR days, if only to get the details straight. In high summer there was what Americans would surely have called 'The Portsmouth Cannon Ball', the 11.35 am from Victoria which, after calling at Clapham Junction, ran the 81½ miles to Fratton in 106 minutes. It only averaged 46 mph but the length of run without a stop was quite exceptional on the 'Brighton' which, in fairness, didn't have the same potential for this sort of thing as other railways. The timetable described this prodigy as 'Fast Train to Portsmouth and Isle of Wight' and it was often worked by D.E. Marsh's economical I3 class 4–4–2 tanks. There was no corresponding up working but then who would want to hurry *away* from the Isle of Wight? In general LSWR services from Waterloo were faster.

The section between Three Bridges and Horsham was older than the Mid-Sussex proper, having been built in 1848 as a branch from the Main Line. It was first extended to Petworth in 1859; four years later a connection from Hardham Junction, south of Pulborough, to the West Coast line between Arundel and Ford was opened. This was part of the LBSCR attempt to regain a respectable share of Portsmouth's traffic, poached by the LSWR in 1859 when it acquired Tom Brassey's speculative Direct Portsmouth Railway. The South Western by and large continued to do best in Portsmouth. Some LBSCR services between London, Bognor and Portsmouth were actually routed via Horsham, Three Bridges and the Main Line. In our own time the creation of Gatwick Airport and a New Town at Crawley have transformed the area of north Sussex between Horsham and Three Bridges.

Lastly I must mention the success story of the Chalk Pits Museum at Amberley. Pepper's Chalk Pits there had, until the 1960s, a rare example in Sussex of an industrial railway system, albeit on a small scale. It was deemed worthy of a visit by enthusiasts whose horizon was usually bounded by the main line railways, by virtue of the strange locomotives employed. Although they have not survived, the site has, and the story of its history and rebirth are given in other Middleton Press books. I could not leave out a taste of its delightful steam power.

81. A rather gloomy old view of the Horsham to Three Bridges 'Motor' arriving at Crawley behind Terrier no. 678 in about 1912. These Motor trains very successfully catered for local traffic during the main part of the working day. They didn't run early or late, nor on Sundays or holidays. A working on this line which diverged from the normal shuttle service was one which started from Midhurst (Mondays only) and another was extended to Horley to set down golfers at Gatwick. (Brighton Library)

82. A more modern view of Crawley's original station, again from the east, showing 'The Wealdsman' railtour passing through in 1965 behind rebuilt Battle of Britain class Pacific no. 34050 *Royal Observer Corps*. (J. Scrace)

83. The old Horsham station is a hive of activity on a summer's day about 1910, seen from the windows of the former West signal box. D1 class 0–4–2 tank no. 265 has stopped with a down train, while on the adjoining track passengers are leaving an up service. Behind the passenger carriages there is a high roofed van and an open truck with a sheeted-over dog-cart loaded on it. Its owners are doubtless relaxing in a First Class compartment further up the train. (Brighton Library)

84. Horsham's new station of 1938 continued to see plenty of steam trains after electrification and this one is waiting in the down loop ready to leave for Brighton. Before the take-over by LSWR M7 class 0–4–4 tanks in 1952, D3 class engines like no. 32364 were the mainstay of this service. (Lens of Sutton)

85. Horsham shed was taking no chances on 10th May 1959. In view of the stiff pull up through Rudgwick that lies ahead, C2X no. 32541 has been coupled on to assist Q class no. 30537 which has brought this Cranleigh-bound excursion down from Victoria. Even so the Q was disabled by Cranleigh and didn't work back in the evening. (J. Scrace)

86. A Horsham - Guildford train crosses the junction at Christ's Hospital in March 1961. By that date push and pull-fitted engines were becoming scarce and the old 'Brighton' motor sets had largely been replaced by 3-coach trains of SR construction. E4 class no. 32578, lacking headcode discs, is carrying lamps on the appropriate irons. (J.H.W. Kent)

87. By March 1961 Christ's Hospital goods yard was on the verge of closure and had no traffic for the Brighton - Horsham train, rattling through at a smart pace behind a 'Vulcan' or C2X class 0–6–0. With the goods safely over Itchingfield Junction the signalman there has cleared both home and distant signals for a down train, as the banner repeaters on the awning show. (J.H.W. Kent)

88. Pulborough's up loop home signal is just being replaced to danger behind the Guard's van as a short Mid-Sussex line goods approaches the loop points. C2X no. 32534 was working out its final mileage in April 1961.

89. Yet another 'Vulcan' goods engine hurrying north on the Mid-Sussex line, is seen from the window of Cray Lane Crossing signal box near Billingshurst in the spring of 1961. Amid the abundance of notices, the economical Southern Railway has reused two made redundant on the LSWR section, warning us to Beware of Trains.

90. D.E. Marsh's attempt to improve on the 'Vulcan' goods in their original (C2) form produced the 'Horsham Goods', class C3. They were few in number and for some reason quite failed their designer, who then produced a most useful type by reboilering the C2s into class C2X. Driver Little has finished shunting at Amberley in 1933 and is attempting the next stage of the Littlehampton - Horsham goods working, a typical C3 job. (F.G. Holmes)

92. The elaborate LBSCR headcode system greatly aided train identification: this is a Portsmouth to Victoria train via Three Bridges and the Main Line. Steam from the safety valves and the injector overflow tells us it is braking to a stop at Arundel. The engine is a B2X rebuild of the spidery B2 class 4–4–0s, no. 314 being altered in 1911, and the mirror finish on the boiler suggests that the labour shortages of World War I have not yet begun. (Lens of Sutton)

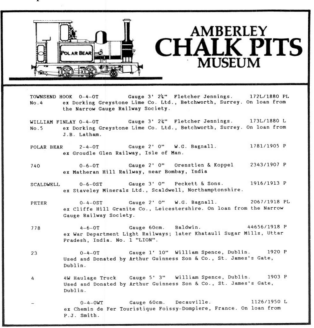

AMBERLEY CHALK PITS MUSEUM

TOWNSEND HOOK No.4	0–4–OT	Gauge 3' 2¼" Fletcher Jennings. ex Dorking Greystone Lime Co. Ltd., Betchworth, Surrey. On loan from the Narrow Gauge Railway Society.	172L/1880 PL	
WILLIAM FINLAY No.5	0–4–OT	Gauge 3' 2¼" Fletcher Jennings. ex Dorking Greystone Lime Co. Ltd., Betchworth, Surrey. On loan from J.B. Latham.	173L/1880 L	
POLAR BEAR	2–4–OT	Gauge 2' 0" W.G. Bagnall. ex Groudle Glen Railway, Isle of Man.	1781/1905 P	
740	0–6–OT	Gauge 2' 0" Orenstien & Koppel ex Matheran Hill Railway, near Bombay, India	2343/1907 P	
SCALDWELL	0–6–OST	Gauge 3' 0" Peckett & Sons. ex Staveley Minerals Ltd., Scaldwell, Northamptonshire.	1916/1913 P	
PETER	0–4–OST	Gauge 2' 0" W.G. Bagnall. ex Cliffe Hill Granite Co., Leicestershire. On loan from the Narrow Gauge Railway Society.	2067/1918 PL	
778	4–6–OT	Gauge 60cm. Baldwin. ex War Department Light Railways; later Khatauli Sugar Mills, Uttar Pradesh, India. No. 1 "LION".	44656/1918 P	
23	0–4–OT	Gauge 1' 10" William Spence, Dublin. Used and Donated by Arthur Guinness Son & Co., St. James's Gate, Dublin.	1920 P	
4	4W Haulage Truck	Gauge 5' 3" William Spence, Dublin. Used and Donated by Arthur Guinness Son & Co., St. James's Gate, Dublin.	1903 P	
–	0–4–OWT	Gauge 60cm. Decauville. ex Chemin de Fer Touristique Foissy-Dompiere, France. On loan from P.J. Smith.	1126/1950 L	

91. Marshall & Co. of Gainsborough were makers of traction engines but in 1878 produced this charming geared undertype 0–4–0 tank. The gearing and access to the machinery prevented the fitting of side tanks in conventional locomotive fashion, and when this engine worked at Pepper's Quarry, Amberley, the water tank was between the frames and surmounted by a substantial steel buffer beam. Wooden brake blocks operated only on the rear wheels. The intruding Hibberd/Planet diesel on the right arrived in 1953 but only lasted four years after the Marshall was scrapped in 1959.

93. The absence of passengers on the platform suggests this London Bridge to Portsmouth train is not booked to stop at Arundel. I3 class no. B30 was the last of the first series, by October 1932 relegated from the hardest duties on the Main Line. (H.C. Casserley)

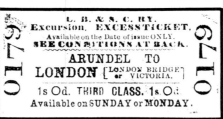

4. BRANCH LINES TO CHRIST'S HOSPITAL

The Cranleigh line was only partly in Sussex and its Surrey stations are shown in my companion volume, *Steaming Through Surrey*. The county boundary runs across the top of Rudgwick tunnel which is still there, an enigma for the explorer. The Sussex end is open though heavily gated but the Surrey end has undergone a curious change. A deepening cutting by which the tracks approached the tunnel mouth has been partly filled in, burying the portal. A curious concrete tower rises out of the weeds and there, at the bottom of it, is the tunnel mouth about 20 feet below. Who did it, and why? The Cranleigh line had only slightly fewer trains than its counterpart, but whether it was the single track, or remoteness from the villages it served, it seemed much more remote and withdrawn. It's on my conscience a little. When country branch lines, even in the prosperous south-east, began to be threatened with closure in the early 1960s, my boss asked me to look at it to see if there was any way we could make economies in its working costs, and perhaps make it 'marginal' in the eyes of the Headquarters Economists, rather than plain 'hopeless'. My chief had experience of saving lines in the West Country by such methods. I'm afraid I was busy with lots of other things and didn't give the Cranleigh line as much attention as I might have. Occasionally I feel guilty that perhaps it could have been saved but I expect that's just wishful thinking. Beeching's axe would have got it in the end.

The Steyning line might have stood a better chance because it was busier, and singling the track would have yielded worthwhile savings. As *Branch Lines to Horsham* (Middleton Press) shows, it was originally single track anyway. Its future would have been as a passenger route, because Southwater brickworks, Steyning market and, after 1981, even Beeding cement works, turned over to road vehicles for their transport needs.

Instead of these 'might have beens', come with a schoolboy and his friend on their first trip over the line. We had discovered the possibility of acquiring relics of the pre-Grouping owners, the LBSCR, in the form of luggage labels printed for that company.

Anything authentically pre-Grouping was much prized and when we began luggage label collecting and found examples easily obtainable we couldn't believe our luck. Country stations were the best sources because they used fewer labels, so one winter's day after school we set off up the Steyning line. With so few trains we could only visit two stations and still get home at a reasonable hour, so we aimed for West Grinstead and Partridge Green. It was dark when we got there, and *country dark*. No street lighting near the stations, just what seemed to two town boys a deep blackness with a few feeble oil lamps. It was as strange to us as we must have been to the solitary porter on duty. "Luggage labels? What do you want those for?" Well, we must have been a persuasive pair, or perhaps he was glad of some company, and in the end we got our labels, as you can see. How strange it was to borrow his oil handlamp for a foray along the unlit platform to visit the 'gents'. I can still remember the return journey, bouncing along in a 'Brighton' motor set through the darkness. The steam heating gurgled and hissed and the faithful D3 tank puffed us along as the generator belt beneath the coach gave out that slight whistling noise characteristic of the LBSCR push and pull sets. It was cold as well as dark now, and the train was an oasis of warmth, light and seemingly life, in the darkness of the winter countryside.

The two branches which converged on Christ's Hospital each had a semi-official name. Although the one going north-west was built as the Horsham & Guildford Direct Railway it was usually called the Cranleigh line. The line going south-east from Christ's Hospital was the Steyning line, both names referring to the most important station on the route. There was another, even less official, name applied to either line depending on the location of the speaker. Somebody in the vicinity of, for example, Guildford, mentioning 'The Linger & Die' would mean the Cranleigh line, contrasting its quietness with the bustle of his own station. Down on the coast at, say, Shoreham, 'The Linger & Die' would mean the Steyning line. I'm sure such a dismissive title must have been used in other places too, to indicate some local and rural railway backwater.

No chapter about these lines would be complete without some detail on the motor trains. The very name, coined about 1905 when 'motor' indicated modernity in the same way 'computer' would today, passed into the local railway language, as 'mail' had done two generations earlier. By using compressed air pumped primarily for train braking (and there was a mighty row with Westinghouse about *that*) the Driver was provided with an easy and reliable method of controlling the engine while he was riding two carriages away at the front of the train. The apparatus on the engines became something of a railway heirloom, passed on from one generation of engines to the next, but by the 1960s it was almost worn out. The old pre-Grouping 2-car sets of pull and push or 'motor fitted' carriages had worn out too, but BR made up some 3-car ones which figure in many of these pictures. The D3 class 0–4–4 tanks were the last LBSCR engines to be 'motor fitted', bequeathing the gear to LSWR M7 and SECR H class tanks. The LMS and BR types of 2–6–2 tanks didn't

bother; they usually ran round the train at the end of each journey. Now that really would have spoiled the 'Double Horsham': one of the pleasantest ways of spending a summer's day that a railway enthusiast could wish for.

It was a Brighton duty, and a real rest cure. Engine pulling, 9.30am Brighton to Horsham. An hour or more sitting quietly there – time for several cups of tea and railway gossip, putting the world straight – then off at 12.21pm pushing to Guildford. Guildford was all bustle and go and foreign territory to Brighton men so we didn't linger there, but set off again after half an hour or so, pulling the train this time and glad to regain the tranquillity of the single line at Peasmarsh Junction. On to Horsham, arriving at 2.33pm and then, after three quarters of an hour, pushing again through a summer afternoon countryside, bound for Brighton reached about 4.30pm, a nice time to book off and finish the day's work. If you can call it work; only the young tearaways who wanted to be out on the Main line complained about being booked for the 'Double Horsham'. I wish you could have come with us.

94. The run down the 1 in 80 gradient from Baynards has left the engine with surplus steam. Too harsh a stop at Rudgwick has caused the boiler water to flood the safety valves and emerge in a shower behind the train. As usual in this line's last years the carriages are an SR corridor composite, an open third, and an SECR 10-compartment 'crowd shifter'. The new platform awning is by BR.

95. H class 0–4–4 tank no. 31530 pushes its train out of Rudgwick through a curve under the bridge and onto the single line towards Slinfold. This bridge accommodated two tracks, the one concealed by the train being the goods yard headshunt. The signal box dates from this century; its tiny predecessor once stood on this side of the line beside the engine.

96. Trains were strengthened to carry crowds of enthusiasts on the last day of services and as the LMS-type 2–6–2 tank arrives at Slinfold from Horsham the photographers are busy capturing the station for their records. Both the restful platform seat and the oil lamps were LBSCR equipment still in use in June 1965. (J.H.W. Kent)

97. Brighton's E4 tank no. 32479 was on the 'Double Horsham' turn of duty this sunny day in March 1961, though not being 'motor fitted' it had to run round its train each trip, three times in all. Here it is just entering the Guildford line platforms at Christ's Hospital with the afternoon train from Guildford. (J.H.W. Kent)

98. The section between Christ's Hospital and Baynards was one of the few on the old LBSCR system where the single line was not controlled by the usual Webb & Thompson electric train staff, but by the older single wooden staff. Here it rests ceremonially on its brackets in Christ's Hospital North signal box. Tickets allowing several trains to follow one another though the section in the same direction with the last one carrying the staff, were kept in the desk. In theory its lock could only be opened by the key in the end of the staff. (J.H.W. Kent)

99. M7 no. 30049 pulls out of the platforms
at Christ's Hospital – there was one on either
side of the train – with the 9.30 am Horsham -
Guildford on 14th April 1954. Before leav-

ing, the Driver will have been given the
wooden single line train staff for the section
to Baynards, which was kept at the signal box
just visible behind the train.

100. The London - Worthing road (A24) crossed the bridge at the north end of South-water station until the recent building of a by-pass for the village, the other bridges in this 1961 picture carrying only lanes. The engine of this Horsham to Brighton train is 2–6–2 tank no. 41301, an LMS design built by BR and used until the diesels came in 1964. (J.H.W. Kent)

102. West Grinstead's station buildings have survived 27 years after this 1960 picture was taken, and are now being renovated. The trains have been gone since 1966 but the Tabby Cat Inn, just peeping over the trees on the right, has recently taken on a new role as a Little Chef. No such luck for M7 no. 30052 or the SECR 1921-built 10 compartment third class behind it. Nature has now taken over the neat platforms and flower beds.

London Brighton & South Coast Railway.

West Grinstead to

E. Grinstead

101. The 1874 signal box figured prominently at the south end of Southwater station but from the late 1950s it was not at all busy, as traffic from the brickworks declined. Once again the train is an LMS-type 2–6–2 tank pulling three SR carriages, the guard's van being in the centre one. (J.H.W. Kent)

2nd · SINGLE	SINGLE 2nd
West Grinstead to	
West Grinstead	West Grinstead
Partridge Green	Partridge Green
PARTRIDGE GREEN	
(8) 6d. FARE 6d. (8)	
For condit'ns see over	For condit'ns see o

2661   2661

103. Partridge Green in July 1959 was still served by a genuine if mixed pre-Grouping train. The engine is LBSCR E4 no. 32468 followed by 2-set no. 653, converted in 1935 for the Allhallows branch in Kent from LSWR carriages built in 1905 and 1899. The last vehicle, completing the pre-Grouping coverage, is a quite modern 1921 SECR third class. How this collection would be prized today. (J.H.W. Kent)

104. Sheet steel has replaced the corridor connection of the 1935 SR brake composite (First and Third class) which was converted into a pull and push driving trailer in 1960 and paired with a 1930 non-compartment or 'open' third class. Next to the M7 pushing the train there is an SECR carriage. The LBSCR is represented by what we can see of Henfield station and the down starting signal, still giving 'line clear' in 1962.

105. This is how we would like to remember Steyning station, complete with everything a country station should have, including the branch train pulling away wreathed in clouds of steam on a February morning. The engine is M7 no. 30050 with an SECR carriage preceding two LBSCR 'bouncers'.

106. Modernisation came to Bramber in April 1957, in the shape of electric light. The afternoon service from Horsham is running true to form: all three pre-Grouping Southern constituents and the SR itself represented in one train. Today even the ground levels have changed here with the building of a by-pass for Bramber and Steyning. No. 30051 would be buried up to its cab roof by what has happened.

London Brighton & South Coast Railway.

Henfield to

Grange Rd.

A a 02727
BR4479
British Railways Board
British Railways (S)
OLD SHOREHAM
BRIDGE TOLL

4d

Receipt for toll paid as per scale exhibited. Available for return on day of issue only. Not transferable. For Conditions see over.

Bell Punch Co., Ltd., London

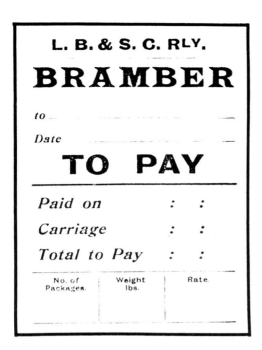

L. B. & S. C. RLY.

BRAMBER

to _____

Date _____

TO PAY

Paid on	:	:
Carriage	:	:
Total to Pay	:	:

No. of Packages.	Weight lbs.	Rate.

Aa 55337

ER4479
British Transport Commission
British Railways (S)

OLD SHOREHAM
BRIDGE TOLL

1d

Receipt for toll paid as
per scale exhibited.
Available for return on
day of issue only.
Not transferable.
For Conditions see over.

Bell Punch Co., Ltd., London

107. In February 1956 the wooden toll bridge over the Adur still carried road traffic which crossed the line by the rear of the train, tolls being collected at the signal box on the left. None of the E4 class 0–6–2 tanks was motor fitted and all had to run round the train at the end of each journey. Thirty years later a single but rusty line of track can still be seen here.

5. THE MIDHURST LINES

108. The southern end of the Chichester - Midhurst line curving away from the West Coast line, as seen from the window of Fishbourne Crossing signal box in September 1964. A goods from Eastleigh is approaching, headed by BR class 4 2-6-0 no. 76054 and signalled into the reception road at Chichester yard.

The little train braked gently to a halt. In the silence the Porter called out "Selham, Selham". And then the Guard: "Selham? Selham? We can't Sel'em, we can't give 'em away". On the other side of the driving compartment the Driver laughed. "He cracks the same joke every time, don't you Bert?" he said to me. There was a gentle chaffing between Porter and Guard. Nobody got in and nobody got out. "That's it then; off you go." The Driver pressed a bell push, at the back of the train a bell rang on the engine, and we pushed away towards Midhurst having done our duty by Selham. Sixteen times a day this ritual was repeated, sometimes the engine pulling the train and sometimes pushing it. I suppose somebody must

have used Selham station, sometime. To me it was always the quietest, and the loneliest, of the stations between Pulborough and Midhurst. Certainly a photographer who got out there to take a picture of the train leaving and was then marooned until it came back, was a welcome visitor to the Porter on duty. Once Selham had been as busy as any small country station but by the early 1950s that was long past. Even Fittleworth seemed to have more life; maybe it was the road bridge close by the station there that made it feel so.

The stations between Chichester and Midhurst I never knew as going concerns. The celebrated washout of 1951 broke the through connection and I went only to Lavant, on a misty autumn day in search of sugar beet with a 'Vulcan' goods. But Midhurst until 1955 was quite a local railway centre, yet only a shadow of what it had been until the 1920s. There were, it is true, long intervals of silence. However, Pulborough - Petersfield services were often timed to cross one another there and for a while there was animation. Then quiet; the railwaymen went back inside to get on with whatever they did in the privacy of their offices and the visiting enthusiast was left to wander around alone, to contemplate the glories of late period LBSCR architecture.

Long after passenger trains had called for the last time we got a letter in the District office enquiring about a suitable site for making part of a film which required 'an antique train'. Midhurst seemed to fill the part to perfection. It wasn't the usual 'drama on a train' that they wanted to make, but a small portion of one of those essentially British creations poking gentle fun at officialdom's pretensions. The hero, ineffectual son of a famous diplomatist father, is sent to a far-off island rent by factional dispute, to try to sort out the mess. His solution is total partition of the island and our little section demonstrated one of the absurdities of this 'white line across everything' approach. The 'plot' showed the partitioners with an outsize pot of white paint dividing the island between the opposing sides regardless of sense. A ruminating cow is partitioned with the white line, and so is a single track railway. The film shows the officials solemnly painting their line into a tunnel from where, after a few seconds, there emerges a train with the white line duly emblazoned on it.

On the appointed day a small army of film people – they never seem to come in groups of less than ten – descended on Midhurst. Fratton shed provided Terrier no. 32640 – old no. 40 *Brighton*, the Gold Medal engine of the 1878 Paris Exhibition – and this with a single coach did duty as the island train. Before filming began it was fitted with a wooden cow-catcher, Old Russian style chimney, and the white rimmed red lamp off the buffer stops. Then it was filmed somewhere out in the country going quietly about its business. Next the whitewash men were filmed painting the line into the tunnel. The engine meanwhile had its broad white stripe painted on, backed into the tunnel, and then emerged before the waiting cameras, suitably partitioned in the cause of island harmony. This activity took all day, cost I know not what, and occupied I suppose ten seconds in the film. It certainly was a better way to spend a sunny day than stuck behind my desk in the office, and it was the last time I saw a train at Midhurst.

109. Late autumn at Lavant in 1957 with C2X no. 32548 cautiously backing onto its train, which is standing at the platform beside the three-storied station. This unusual building avoided the need for a steep station approach road.

110. The southern end of West Dean tunnel seen from the footplate, as the engine barks its way up the 1 in 75 gradient towards Singleton station which lies beyond the wooded ridge. Today the line here is a rough road leading to the premises of Messrs. Singleton Joinery which occupy the cutting and a little of the tunnel, the other end being boarded up. (Brighton Library)

111. A slow speed derailment on the low embankment north of Cocking station left D1 tank no. 239 *Patcham* not en route for Midhurst but completely off the rails together with its trucks and Guard's Van no. 260. The two LBSCR steam cranes were summoned from New Cross and Brighton and after several attempts they restored *Patcham* to its proper place on the rails. On the Sunday afternoon of 11th September 1904 the local crowd had a free show they would long remember. (Brighton Library)

112. Rogate was the previous stop for M7 class no. 30046, which blows off as it arrives at Elsted in November 1954. The bridge could accommodate double track if needed, but so far as is known there was never any loop here. (R.C. Riley)

113. The end of Fittleworth's wooden building was adorned in 1954 with two of those vanished delights, poster time-tables. Generations of railwaymen cursed as they tried to rule a straight line across them below the times shown for trains to call at their own station. The trick was to do it on the Waiting Room table *before* pasting it up on the board. As usual in the last years of the Midhurst line the engine of this Pulborough-bound train is an M7.

114. A rumbling of wheels, a hiss of steam, and exchanged greetings between train crew and station staff briefly disturbed Petworth's quiet this April Saturday in 1954. The signalman has already got 'line clear' from Hardham Junction and taken a single line staff from the machine in the signal box to give to the driver. He has also cleared the starting signal, an SR upper quadrant arm on an LBSCR wooden post.

115. Selham's platform nameboard was of concrete in the early SR style. Unusually the name was repeated on both the front and the side of the 'Gents'. Notice the array of chimneys and pots on this simple building: in 1872 passengers expected a fire in the Waiting Room as they congregated there on wet days, in the absence of a platform awning.

116. Midhurst station as seen from the driving compartment of a motor train, with the LBSCR home signal at clear. The signalling gives no indication as to which platform the train will use. There were once sidings on both sides of the line here.

117. Moving up to the station itself we see the Pulborough train waiting to leave behind the usual M7, no. 30050. The starting signal was no longer operated from the South signal box on the right, which the Station Master had taken over as his office in 1925.

118. The scene at Midhurst station in August 1958 before the film crew arrived to make 'Carleton-Browne of the F.O.'. But for the Area Inspector's car on the platform and the unusual motive power, this picture could have been taken when the passenger service was still running.

119. After the make-up artists had done their worst to no. 32640 it was ready to back into the tunnel and then reappear as the cameras rolled. Railway staff are outnumbered about 10 to 1. Today this spot is the back garden of a block of flats but the tunnel is still there with wooden doors on this end.

120. This mid-day working over the Petersfield - Midhurst section was a one coach motor train, by no means a common practice. There were a few of these single driving trailers for work such as this, and to strengthen a two coach motor train so that the engine pushed one and pulled two. M7 no. 30246 was on duty in April 1954.

6. SELSEY TRAMWAY

121. The Hundred of Manhood & Selsey Tramway was in a class of its own, having been engineered and managed by the King of Light Railways – the inimitable Colonel Holman Fred Stephens. The line was renamed the West Sussex Railway in 1924 and ceased operation in 1935. This Manning Wardle 0–6–0ST *Ringing Rock* was typical of the motley assortment of locomotives provided for the almost level line from Chichester to Selsey. This strange photograph was taken at Selsey Town (the village had three stations – see *Branch Line to Selsey*) and shows an early experiment to reduce steam in West Sussex. Partly in the shed is the Wolseley-Siddeley petrol railcar which, unlike the later cars, was not one of a pair. To haul it back to Chichester this Ford Model T lorry was provided. One headlight and the steering wheel had been retained! The latter is just visible, as the vehicle was left hand drive, having been built in the USA. (Col. Stephens Rly. Museum, Tenterden)

MP Middleton Press

Easebourne Lane, Midhurst, West Sussex, GU29 9AZ
☎ Midhurst (073 081) 3169

BRANCH LINES

BRANCH LINES TO MIDHURST	0 906520 01 0
BRANCH LINES TO HORSHAM	0 906520 02 9
BRANCH LINE TO SELSEY	0 906520 04 5
BRANCH LINES TO EAST GRINSTEAD	0 906520 07 X
BRANCH LINES TO ALTON	0 906520 11 8
BRANCH LINE TO HAYLING	0 906520 12 6
BRANCH LINE TO SOUTHWOLD	0 906520 15 0
BRANCH LINE TO TENTERDEN	0 906520 21 5
BRANCH LINES TO NEWPORT	0 906520 26 6
BRANCH LINES TO TUNBRIDGE WELLS	0 906520 32 0
BRANCH LINE TO SWANAGE	0 906520 33 9
BRANCH LINES AROUND GOSPORT	0 906520 36 3
BRANCH LINES TO LONGMOOR	0 906520 41 X
BRANCH LINE TO LYME REGIS	0 906520 45 2
BRANCH LINES AROUND MIDHURST	0 906520 49 5

SOUTH COAST RAILWAYS

BRIGHTON TO WORTHING	0 906520 03 7
WORTHING TO CHICHESTER	0 906520 06 1
CHICHESTER TO PORTSMOUTH	0 906520 14 2
BRIGHTON TO EASTBOURNE	0 906520 16 9
RYDE TO VENTNOR	0 906520 19 3
EASTBOURNE TO HASTINGS	0 906520 27 4
PORTSMOUTH TO SOUTHAMPTON	0 906520 31 2
HASTINGS TO ASHFORD	0 906520 37 1
SOUTHAMPTON TO BOURNEMOUTH	0 906520 42 8

SOUTHERN MAIN LINES

WOKING TO PORTSMOUTH	0 906520 25 8
HAYWARDS HEATH TO SEAFORD	0 906520 28 2
EPSOM TO HORSHAM	0 906520 30 4
CRAWLEY TO LITTLEHAMPTON	0 906520 34 7
THREE BRIDGES TO BRIGHTON	0 906520 35 5
WATERLOO TO WOKING	0 906520 38 X
VICTORIA TO EAST CROYDON	0 906520 40 1
TONBRIDGE TO HASTINGS	0 906520 44 4

STEAMING THROUGH

STEAMING THROUGH KENT	0 906520 13 4
STEAMING THROUGH EAST HANTS	0 906520 18 5
STEAMING THROUGH EAST SUSSEX	0 906520 22 3
STEAMING THROUGH SURREY	0 906520 39 8

OTHER RAILWAY BOOKS

WAR ON THE LINE The official history of the SR in World War II	0 906520 10 X
GARRAWAY FATHER AND SON The story of two careers in steam	0 906520 20 7

OTHER BOOKS

MIDHURST TOWN – THEN & NOW	0 906520 05 3
EAST GRINSTEAD – THEN & NOW	0 906520 17 7
THE MILITARY DEFENCE OF WEST SUSSEX	0 906520 23 1
WEST SUSSEX WATERWAYS	0 906520 24 X
BATTLE OVER PORTSMOUTH A City at war in 1940	0 906520 29 0